Love to Dance

Ballroom

Angela Royston

Raintree is an imprint of Capstone Global Library Limited, a company incorporated in England and Wales having its registered office at 7 Pilgrim Street, London, EC4V 6LB – Registered company number: 6695582

To contact Raintree:
Phone: 0845 6044371
Fax: + 44 (0) 1865 312263
Email: myorders@raintreepublishers.co.uk
Outside the UK please telephone +44 1865 312262.

Text © Capstone Global Library Limited 2013
First published in hardback in 2013

The moral rights of the proprietor have been asserted.

Edited by Nancy Dickmann, Catherine Veitch, and Abby Colich
Designed by Cynthia Della-Rovere
Picture research by Elizabeth Alexander
Production by Alison Parsons
Originated by Capstone Global Library Ltd
Printed and bound in China by CTPS

ISBN 978 1 406 24947 7
16 15 14 13 12
10 9 8 7 6 5 4 3 2 1

British Library Cataloguing in Publication Data
Royston, Angela
Ballroom. -- (Love to dance)
793.3'3-dc23
A full catalogue record for this book is available from the British Library.

Acknowledgements
We would like to thank the following for permission to reproduce photographs: Alamy pp. 6 (© North Wind Picture Archives), 13 (© ZUMA Wire Service), 17 (© Zbigniew Tomaszewski), 20 (© tarczas), 21 (© tarczas), 22 (© Jeff Gilbert), 23 (© Pictorial Press Ltd), 25 (© Geoff A Howard), 26 (© RIA Novosti); Corbis pp. 7 (© Bettmann), 12 (© Michael Ochs Archives), 14 (© yangzongyou/Xinhua Press), 24 (© Ilian Iliev/Lebrecht Music & Arts), 28 (© Pittsburgh Post-Gazette/ZUMA Press); Getty Images pp. 8 (DEA / A. DAGLI ORTI), 10 (Pailin Wedel/Raleigh News & Observer/MCT), 27 (Photo by 20th Century-Fox), 29 (Per-Anders Pettersson); iStockphoto p. 18 (© Oleg Filipchuk); Shutterstock pp. 5 (© akva), 9 (© Zzvet), 11 (© Igor Bulgarin), 16 (© Anky); SuperStock title page (© Blend Images), 4 (© Fancy Collection), 15 (© age footstock), 19 (© Prisma).

Design features reproduced with permission of Shutterstock (© Nejron Photo, © Roman Sigaev).

Front cover photograph of ballroom dancers reproduced with permission of Shutterstock (© Zzvet).

We would like to thank Allen Desterhaft for his invaluable help in the preparation of this book.

Every effort has been made to contact copyright holders of material reproduced in this book. Any omissions will be rectified in subsequent printings if notice is given to the publisher.

Contents

Some words are shown in bold, **like this**. You can find out what they mean by looking in the glossary.

This is ballroom dancing!

Two dancers glide together across the floor. She is wearing high heels and a glamorous dress. Their feet move in perfect time to the music. They are taking part in a competition for ballroom dancers, called **dancesport**.

What is it all about?

Cheryl Burke, a ballroom dance teacher says, "Ballroom to me was so exciting – the music, the costumes…"

Where ballroom began

Ballroom dancing began in royal palaces and the large houses of rich people. That is why ballroom dancers today still wear **formal** suits and fancy ball gowns.

The Minuet

The Minuet was a popular ballroom dance in 1800. The dancers followed set moves and steps as they moved from one partner to the next.

Waltzing

After 1800, people began to dance a new dance, the Viennese **Waltz**. Each couple danced close together and stayed together for the whole dance. Today, two waltzes are danced – the Viennese and the Slow Waltz.

This painting shows couples dancing the Viennese Waltz.

How shocking!

In the 1800s, many people disapproved of waltzing. They thought it was wrong for a man and woman to dance so close together!

Take your partners...

In ballroom dancing, a man and a woman dance together as partners. **Dancesport** partners spend many hours practising their dance moves. They want to dance perfectly in the next competition!

The closed hold

Each dance usually begins with the dance partners standing in the closed hold. This hold helps them to keep time together.

The jazz age

In the early 1900s, ballroom dancers began dancing to **jazz**. This exciting style of music was invented by African Americans. It led to many different dances, including the **Lindy Hop**.

The Lindy Hop

The most famous Lindy Hopper was Frankie Manning. He introduced spectacular moves, such as flipping his partner over his head!

Dance style: the Quickstep

The **Quickstep** is a popular ballroom dance. The dancers move quickly and lightly around the floor. The dance is made up of a slow step followed by two quick steps, and then another slow step.

Hops and twirls

The two quick steps allow the
dancers to twirl, hop, skip, and
spin. They look as if they are flying!

What to wear

Women and girls' dresses are often covered with sequins, feathers, or sparkling rhinestones, which look like diamonds. Women wear high-heeled shoes.

Dressed to impress!

Men often wear suits and leather shoes. The suit can be very **formal** with **long tails**, or it can be specially designed for the dance.

17

Dance style: the Tango

The **Tango** is one of the best-known dances. The dancers stand upright and then walk together forwards, backwards, or to the side. This is called the promenade.

Eye-catching

The dancers may pause between one sequence of steps and the next. During the pause, the woman takes up a **dramatic**, eye-catching position.

19

Competitive ballroom

In competitions, ballroom dances are divided into standard ballroom and Latin ballroom. The standard ballroom dances are the **Quickstep**, the Foxtrot, the Slow **Waltz**, the **Tango**, and the Viennese Waltz.

Latin ballroom

The Latin dances are the Cha Cha Cha, Samba, Rumba, Paso Doble, and the Jive. In Latin ballroom, the dancers often dance further apart.

Dance style: the Jive

The Jive includes twists and turns with the dancers changing position. In **dancesport**, the basic step is two rocking steps and then three small steps to each side.

The Cake Walk

Jive competitions began around the 1880s. The dance was called the Cake Walk, because the prize was a cake.

And the winner is...

Today, few young people dance ballroom dances, except in competitions. **Dancesport** is popular in many countries. In wheelchair dancesport, one of the partners uses a wheelchair.

Biggest competition

The biggest international competition is held every year in Blackpool in the UK. Dancers from about 50 countries take part.

Where to see ballroom dancing

You do not have to go far to see ballroom dancing. There are several programmes on television. In some, a professional dancer works with a celebrity.

Dance programmes are seen around the world. This version of *Dancing with the Stars* was shown on Russian television.

Dance films

Several films are about ballroom dancing.
In the 1940s and 1950s, Fred Astaire was a
leading star. Above, he dances with Leslie
Caron in the film *Daddy Long Legs*.

Give it a go!

Ballroom is fun to watch, but it is even better to dance. Look for classes for children in your neighbourhood. You just need some comfy clothes.

A new you

Dancing is a good way to exercise and to make friends. Dancing will help you to feel more confident about yourself.

Glossary

dancesport ballroom dancing performed in a competition, rather than just for fun

dramatic describes something that stands out and catches your attention

formal smart, according to a set of rules

jazz type of music that has strong rhythm and allows musicians to play the music as they like

Lindy Hop style of dance that began in New York, USA. It was danced to jazz music.

long tails formal jacket that is short at the front but has two long "tails" at the back

Quickstep standard ballroom dance in which the dancers spin, run, and jump around the dance floor

Tango romantic standard ballroom dance that began in Argentina

waltz the first standard ballroom dance. It has two forms, the Viennese Waltz, which came from Austria in the 1800s, and the Slow Waltz, which began in the 1920s.

Find out more

Books

Ballroom (Xtreme Dance), S. Hamilton (ABDO & Daughters, 2011)

Ballroom Dancing (Culture in Action), Deborah Underwood (Raintree, 2009)

Ballroom Dancing (Snap Books), Joan Freese (Capstone Press, 2007)

Ballroom Dancing for Fun, Jennifer Blizin Gillis (Compass Point Books, 2008)

Websites

www.dance4sport.net/site
This website has lots of information about dancing, including learning to dance, and competitions such as Blackpool International Dance Festival.

www.learntodance.com/online%20Ballroom.htm
This video clip shows you how to do the closed hold, which is the starting position for ballroom dancing.

Index